CONTENTS

STROLLING DOWN MEMORY LANE IN "THE HAPPIEST PLACE ON EARTH"

"Disneyland will never be completed as long as there is imagination left in the world"

Walt Disney

1955

▶ After more than 20 years of planning and dreaming, Walt Disney opens the original Disney theme park, Disneyland® Park, to a curious world on Sunday, July 17, 1955.

During its first year of operation, Disneyland presents the following attractions in five themed lands:

Main Street, USA
- Disneyland Railroad
- Horse-drawn Street Cars
- Horse-drawn Fire Wagon
- Main Street Cinema
- Horse-drawn Surreys
- Main Street Penny Arcade
- Main Street Shooting Gallery

Adventureland
- Jungle Cruise

Fantasyland
- King Arthur Carrousel
- Peter Pan Flight
- Mr. Toad's Wild Ride
- Canal Boats of the World
- Snow White's Adventures
- Casey Jr. Circus Train
- Dumbo the Flying Elephant
- Mickey Mouse Club Theater
- Mickey Mouse Club Circus
- Mad Tea Party

Frontierland
- Stage Coach
- Mule Pack
- Mark Twain Riverboat
- Golden Horseshoe Revue
- Davy Crockett Museum
- Conestoga Wagons
- Mike Fink Keel Boats

Tomorrowland
- Tomorrowland Autopia
- Space Station X-1
- Circarama, USA (360-degree film, *A Tour of the West*)
- Monsanto Hall of Chemistry
- Rocket to the Moon
- Phantom Boats
- Color Gallery
- The World Beneath Us
- 20,000 Leagues Under the Sea
- Tomorrowland Flight Circle
- Aluminum Hall of Fame

▶ On September 8, after only seven weeks of operation, Disneyland welcomes Elsa Marquez as its one millionth guest.

1956

▶ The "Fantasy in the Sky" fireworks spectacular is introduced

▶ 15 new attractions are added to Disneyland:
- Astro Jets
- Bathroom of Tomorrow
- Storybook Land Canal Boats
- Tom Sawyer Island Rafts
- Skyway to Tomorrowland and Skyway to Fantasyland
- Horseless Carriages (red and yellow)
- Rainbow Ridge Pack Mules
- Rainbow Mountain
- Stage Coach
- Rainbow Caverns
- Mine Train
- Main Street Omnibus
- Indian Village
- Indian War Canoes
- Junior Autopia

1957

▶ Nine new attractions are added to Disneyland:
- Midget Autopia
- Sleeping Beauty Castle (walk-through attraction)
- Holidayland
- Monsanto House of the Future
- Viewliner
- Motor Boat Cruise
- Indian Village Rafts
- Frontierland Shooting Gallery
- Main Street Omnibus

1958

▶ Four new attractions are added to Disneyland:
- Grand Canyon Diorama
- Alice in Wonderland
- Columbia Sailing Ship
- Motorized Main Street Fire Truck

1959

▶ Four new attractions are added to Disneyland:
- Fantasyland Autopia
- Submarine Voyage
- Disneyland-Alweg Monorail System
- Matterhorn Bobsleds

▶ Disneyland greets its 15 millionth guest in April.

1960

▶ Six new attractions are added to Disneyland:
- Main Street Electric Cars
- Art of Animation Exhibit
- Mine Train Through Nature's Wonderland
- Skull Rock
- Pirate's Cove
- New Circarama film *America the Beautiful*

▶ "Dixieland at Disneyland" debuts on the Rivers of America in Frontierland.

1961

▶ Four new attractions are added to Disneyland:
- Snow White Grotto & Wishing Well
- Monorail to Disneyland Hotel
- Flying Saucers
- Babes in Toyland Exhibit

▶ First all-night Grad Nite Party for high school graduates is held at Disneyland in June.

1962

▶ Four new attractions are added to Disneyland:
- Safari Shooting Gallery
- Indian Village (expansion)
- Jungle Cruise (new scenes added)
- Swiss Family Treehouse

1963

▶ The debut of Walt Disney's Enchanted Tiki Room in Adventureland marks a new era in Disneyland attractions by introducing a new form of three-dimensional animation called Audio-Animatronics®.

▶ The "Parade of Toys" becomes a daily feature during the Christmas holiday.

▶ "Salute to Mexico," a cultural exhibit, is presented by People-to-People and the Mexican Tourist Association.

▶ Disneyland showcases its first "Cavalcade of Big Bands," a series of concerts by some of the biggest names in swing music.

1966

▶ Three major new attractions are added to Disneyland:

● "it's a small world"
● Primeval World Diorama
● New Orleans Square

▶ In July, Walt Disney dedicates the first new land since the opening of Disneyland: New Orleans Square. This three-acre, $18 million dollar expansion captures the charm of the "Paris of the American Frontier" as it was during the early part of the 18th century.

1965

▶ The first Disneyland Ambassador to the World, Julie Reihm (chosen in 1964), represents Disneyland® Park on goodwill tours to Europe, Canada, Australia, New Zealand, Japan, and throughout the United States.

▶ Great Moments with Mr. Lincoln becomes the first Disney show from the 1964-65 New York World's Fair to be transplanted to Disneyland. The show finds a new home in the Main Street Opera House.

1964

▶ On May 17, "Disneyland Goes to the World's Fair" airs for the first time on Disney's Sunday night TV series *The Wonderful World of Color*. Hosted by Walt Disney, the episode highlights the four Disney shows in the 1964-65 New York World's Fair.

▶ Two new additions are made to Disneyland:

● Columbia Sailing Ship (below decks museum)
● Jungle Cruise (new scenes added)

1967

▶ Seven major new attractions are added to Disneyland:

● Pirates of the Caribbean
● Circle-Vision featuring *America the Beautiful*
● Carousel of Progress
● PeopleMover
● Rocket Jets
● Flight to the Moon
● Adventure Thru Inner Space

▶ In July, 1,500 celebrities and invited guests attend the dedication of an all-new Tomorrowland, revamped at a cost of $23 million. "A World on the Move," Tomorrowland adds six new attractions to the Disneyland landscape.

1968

▶ Special events for the year include the park's first St. Patrick's Day Parade, first Cinco de Mayo Fiesta, plus a Valentine's Day Party, Spring Fling, Easter Parade, and Angels-Disneyland Fun Day Doubleheader.

1971

▶ On October 1, the Walt Disney World® Resort in Florida is officially dedicated and opened by Roy O. Disney (Walt Disney's brother and lifelong business partner). This new venture in Disney outdoor entertainment is built upon the successful blueprint of Disneyland. Numerous Disneyland cast members in California contribute to the creation and opening of the Walt Disney World Resort.

▶ Miss Valerie Suldo, a 22-year-old New Brunswick, New Jersey payroll clerk, becomes Disneyland Guest Number 100 million at 11:13 A.M. on Thursday, June 17, 1971, launching a summer-long celebration.

1970

▶ On July 17, 130 of the original Disneyland staff, known as Club 55, gather for a special celebration. Combined, the total service to Disneyland guests of these very special cast members is more than 1,950 years!

1969

▶ On August 9, Disneyland officially opens the doors to The Haunted Mansion, one of the park's most beloved attractions.

▶ "Love Bug Day" is celebrated at Disneyland on March 23rd with the convergence of hundreds of Volkswagens.

▶ The landing of Apollo 11, on July 20, on the surface of the moon is televised from the Tomorrowland Stage to a throng of fascinated Disneyland guests. This is a historic milestone for Disneyland as well as the world.

▶ One new attraction is added to Disneyland:

● Davy Crockett's Explorer Canoes (redesigned)

1972

▶ Disneyland debuts its seventh themed land with the opening of Bear Country and the addition of the following attractions:

● Country Bear Jamboree
● Teddi Bara's Swingin' Arcade

▶ The beloved "Disneyland Main Street Electrical Parade" premiers at Disneyland and quickly becomes the most popular parade ever staged at a Disney theme park.

1974

▶ America Sings debuts on June 28 in Tomorrowland's Carousel Theater. This comical, lively, and tune-filled musical showcases nearly 200 years of our nation's musical heritage.

▶ On July 11, 1974, Disneyland is the star of the nationally televised TV special *Herbie Day at Disneyland*.

1973

▶ Two new attractions are added to Disneyland:

● The Walt Disney Story
● Disneyland Showcase

▶ In April, Mrs. Lillian Bounds Disney (Mrs. Walt Disney) officiates at the grand opening of The Walt Disney Story at the Main Street Opera House on Main Street, USA. This impressive and emotional salute to Walt Disney and his creative legacy features exacting recreations of his studio offices, displays of his many awards, and demonstrations of Audio-Animatronics®.

1975

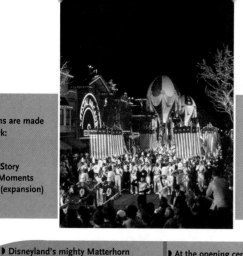

▶ Two new additions are made to Disneyland® Park:

● Mission to Mars
● The Walt Disney Story Featuring Great Moments with Mr. Lincoln (expansion)

▶ Conceived as a salute and celebration in honor of the American Bicentennial, "America on Parade" begins its daily performances in July, 1975, at both Disneyland and at the Walt Disney World Resort, and continues until September, 1976. In all, the red-white-and-blue procession completes more than 1,200 performances before a total audience of 25 million guests, the largest audience ever to view a live performance.

1976

▶ On June 22, Elsie Mae Houck of Tulare, California, becomes Disneyland's 150 millionth guest.

▶ Disneyland is the star of two nationally televised TV specials: *Monsanto presents Walt Disney's America on Parade,* starring comedian Red Skelton and airing on April 3, 1976; and *Christmas in Disneyland,* starring actor-comedian Art Carney and airing on December 6, 1976 (this special is famous for its spectacular ice-skating sequence on Main Street, USA).

1978

▶ Disneyland's mighty Matterhorn Bobsleds receives a major renovation which results in the addition of ice caverns, glowing ice crystals, and the ever-threatening Abominable Snowman.

▶ On November 18–19, Mickey's Official 50th Birthday Party is attended by more than 91,762 guests! On hand for the festivities are the original members of *The Mickey Mouse Club.*

1977

▶ At the opening ceremonies of Space Mountain on May 27, Disneyland is honored to have as special guests America's first men in space—the U.S. Mercury Astronauts:

● Scott Carpenter
● Wally Schirra
● U.S. Senator John Glenn
● Betty Grissom, widow of Virgil I. "Gus" Grissom

● Gordon Cooper
● Alan Shepard
● Donald "Deke" Slayton

1982

▶ Beginning in June, the Disneyland Passport, good for admission and unlimited use of park attractions, becomes the exclusive ticket media for the park. With the introduction of the Passport, the venerable Disneyland Ticket Book and its famous A, B, C, D, and E ticket coupons is officially retired.

▶ In July, the Disneyland Marching Band celebrates its 50,000th performance for Disneyland guests.

1985

▶ Two new additions are made to Disneyland:

● Frontierland Shootin' Arcade
● Videopolis

▶ In January, Disneyland kicks off a yearlong celebration of "30 Years of Magic" with daily shows and special parades.
▶ On February 2, the nationally televised TV special *Disneyland's 30th Anniversary Celebration* showcases 30 years of Disneyland.
▶ On February 6, for the first time in its history, Disneyland begins year-round, seven-days-a-week operation.
▶ On August 4, Disneyland welcomes its 250 millionth guest, Brooks Charles Arthur Burr, 3, of Anchorage, Alaska.

1979

▶ On a busy July 4, near Main Street, USA, Teresa Salcedo is born to Rosa and Elias Salcedo of Los Angeles, California. Mickey Mouse later presents little Teresa with Disneyland Birth Certificate No. 1, recognizing the unprecedented event.
▶ In September, Big Thunder Mountain Railroad opens in Frontierland. Replacing the Mine Train Through Nature's Wonderland, the new attraction covers two acres. Huge cranes were used to hoist the complete upper buttes (weighing up to 28 tons) into position atop the massive steel framework.

1981

▶ On January 8, at 11:00 A.M., Gert Schelvis, 26, of Santa Barbara, California, becomes the 200 millionth guest to visit Disneyland.

1980

▶ In January, Disneyland begins its yearlong silver anniversary celebration in grand style with a daily parade, "Disneyland's 25th Anniversary Parade," and the popular stage show "Disneyland is Your Land."

1983

▶ On May 25, an all-new redesigned Fantasyland is unveiled in a spectacular grand opening, including a ceremonial lowering of the Sleeping Beauty Castle drawbridge (an event not seen since the opening day of Disneyland 28 years earlier). The new Fantasyland features new versions of favorite attractions and new landmarks such as:

● Pinocchio's Daring Journey
● Snow White's Scary Adventures
● Peter Pan's Flight
● Mr. Toad's Wild Ride
● Dumbo the Flying Elephant
● The Sword in the Stone
● Mad Tea Party
● King Arthur Carrousel

1984

▶ Three major new attractions are added to Disneyland:

● Alice In Wonderland (redesign)
● Magic Journeys
● Country Bear Christmas Show

1986

▶ Three major new attractions are added to Disneyland:

● Country Bear Vacation Hoedown
● Big Thunder Ranch
● Magic Eye Theater (featuring *Captain EO*)

▶ Summer sees a total of 1,320 Disneyland cast members and Disney characters join hands in the coast-to-coast charity fundraising effort "Hands Across America."

1992

▶ On May 13, Fantasmic!, a new tradition in Disneyland nighttime entertainment, premiers on the Rivers of America in Frontierland. This hugely popular evening extravaganza features a battle of good and evil inside Mickey Mouse's fanciful imagination.

1993

▶ On January 26, Disneyland celebrates the grand opening of Mickey's Toontown, a new addition to Fantasyland. This new area features the following attractions:

- Mickey's House and Movie Barn
- Minnie's House and Garden
- Donald's Boat: The *Miss Daisy*
- Goofy's Bounce House
- Gadget's Go-Coaster
- Jolly Trolley
- Chip 'n Dale's Treehouse

1994

▶ The fun-filled attraction Roger Rabbit's Car Toon Spin officially opens in Mickey's Toontown on January 26.

1991

▶ In March, Small World Mall is magically transformed into "Disney Afternoon Avenue." Teeming with new sights and sounds, "Disney Afternoon Avenue" gives children a colorful play area in which they can interact with their favorite stars from *The Disney Afternoon* TV series. Highlights include the "Plane Crazy" stage show at Videopolis, and a chance to meet its star, Baloo, in his dressing room.

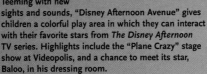

1990

▶ The 35th anniversary of Disneyland is marked by the premiere of the "Party Gras Parade," featuring wild and fun Cajun beats and six 37-foot-tall Disney character inflatable balloon floats.

1999

▶ On May 20, Disneyland hosts the official homecoming of Army Staff Sergeant Andrew Ramirez, Staff Sergeant Christopher Stone, and Specialist Steven Gozales. It is the first time the three U.S. soldiers, who had been captured by Serbian forces on March 31, saw each other since their release from captivity.

• Tarzan's Treehouse™ opens in Adventureland on June 23 (replacing the Swiss Family Treehouse).

1998

▶ Michael Eisner, officially dedicates the new Tomorrowland, along with 40 past and present U.S. Astronauts, on Thursday, May 21.

2001

▶ On February 8, Disney's California Adventure Park opens with three districts: Golden State, Hollywood Pictures Backlot, and Paradise Pier. Downtown Disney, a mecca for shopping, dining, and entertainment opens on January 12

2000

▶ In January, Disneyland kicks off a yearlong celebration of its 45th birthday.

1997

1996

▶ "it's a small world" Holiday premiers on November 27. This all-new winter holiday-theme overlay to the classic Disneyland attraction "it's a small world" highlights winter holiday festivities around the world and intertwines "Deck the Halls" and "Jingle Bells" with the attraction's famous theme song.

1989

▶ On July 17, Splash Mountain, the most elaborate flume attraction in the world, opens to Disneyland guests. Located in Critter Country (formerly Bear Country), the towering 87-foot-tall Splash Mountain adventure culminates in a breathtaking five-story drop at a 45-degree angle. Splash Mountain is based upon the animated sequences of Walt Disney's classic 1946 film *Song of the South*.

1988

▶ Mickey's 60th birthday is celebrated daily during the summer with "Mickey's 60th Birthday Parade" and "Mickey's Birthday Bash" in the Plaza Hub.

1995

▶ In February, the biggest attraction ever created for a Disney theme park—The Indiana Jones™ Adventure—is unveiled during a star-studded opening gala.

▶ Springtime sees the transformation of Big Thunder Ranch into the medieval setting of "The Hunchback of Notre Dame Festival of Fools." This popular stage show, presented in the round, is derived from the Disney animated film *The Hunchback of Notre Dame.*

1987

▶ Two major new attractions are added to Disneyland® Park:

- Star Tours
- The Disney Gallery

▶ On January 12, Star Tours, the first attraction collaboration between Disney and Lucasfilm, Ltd., premieres in Tomorrowland.

▶ On May 5, Disney Dollars are

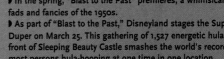

unveiled at Disneyland. This unique currency, with equivalent value to U.S. currency, is introduced for use at the Disney theme parks and resorts. Mickey Mouse appears on the $1 bill and Goofy on the $5 bill. A $10 bill featuring Minnie Mouse is added on November 20, 1989.

▶ In the spring, "Blast to the Past" premieres, a whimsical look at the fads and fancies of the 1950s.

▶ As part of "Blast to the Past," Disneyland stages the Super Hooper Duper on March 25. This gathering of 1,527 energetic hula-hoopers in front of Sleeping Beauty Castle smashes the world's record for the most persons hula-hooping at one time in one location.

DISNEY'S CALIFORNIA ADVENTURE™ PARK

The grandeur, lore, and energy of California find an exciting

showcase in Disney's California Adventure Park. Unveiled in

2001, this spectacular 55-acre theme park is the

largest addition to the Disneyland Resort

since Disneyland Park itself opened in 1955.

California's majestic

landscapes, rich cultural history, and electric

lifestyle are celebrated in a panorama of fun-filled attractions,

stirring entertainments, and colorful parades, as wondrous

adventures transport guests through times past, present, and

future. Disney Magic meets California fun

in a park that is as diverse and full

of surprises as the land that

inspired it.

Entry and Sunshine Plaza

As guests enter the park, they walk under a scale representation of San Francisco's Golden Gate Bridge. Instead of cars, the monorails traverse the aptly named "Golden State Bridge" between two 58-foot towers (opposite page).

C-A-L-I-F-O-R-N-I-A, proclaimed in letters eleven-and-a-half feet high, marks the entryway into Disney's California Adventure Park (right).

The entry to Disney's California Adventure Park resembles a picture-postcard view of all the fun, sun, and excitement California has to offer, in a uniquely designed landscape. After passing through tall sculptures spelling "CALIFORNIA," guests pass by a mosaic tile mural portraying the topographical beauty of the state.

The journey continues as guests stroll under a replica of the Golden Gate Bridge along which the Disneyland Monorail glides. A recreation of the legendary Western Pacific California Zephyr, the luxurious train that brought millions of travelers to California after World War II, stands regally at the entrance to Sunshine Plaza.

As the portal to the major areas of Disney's California Adventure Park, Sunshine Plaza is a prime spot to catch a parade, enjoy the quintessential California shopping experience, savor a sweet selection of West-Coast confections, or relax by a refreshing fountain.

Sunshine Plaza

Shining above a wave fountain is a radiant sun, standing more than 50 feet high and covered in ultra-thin titanium. It projects a sunny glow reflected from six heliostatic mirrors that rotate to follow the sun throughout the day. This shimmering icon serves as the hub of the park, and Sunshine Plaza marks the branching-off point for each of the lands in Disney's California Adventure.

SHOPPING AND DINING AT SUNSHINE PLAZA

At Greetings from California, where you can find "Everything Under the Sun," guests can purchase souvenirs and mementoes. Engine-Ears Toys, a unique, over-sized model train "fantasy world," features innovative, interactive toys and tempting, tasty goodies.

Baker's Field Bakery is a premier patisserie-style bakery brimming with the rich aroma of gourmet coffees, cappuccinos, and savory pastries. On the outside it looks like a powerful locomotive; inside it's reminiscent of an old downtown train station. Bur-r-r-bank Ice Cream offers a chillingly great selection of the finest-quality ice cream, waffle cones, and sundaes.

Entry Mosaic

A pair of mosaics with 12,000 hand-cast tiles depict snowcapped peaks, breaking waves, and majestic forests, to create a three-dimensional montage of California landmarks that beckons guests into this exciting new park.

Disney on Parade

Disney's Eureka! A California Parade (right) celebrates the cultural diversity of California in a colorful and entertaining extravaganza. A pageant of nearly 100 performers, puppets, and towering parade units weaves its way around the park, making performance stops where guests can interact with the theatrical experience. With more than half-a-million light bulbs sparkling in a procession over a quarter-mile long, Disney's Electrical Parade (left and below) offers dazzling fun. Its brilliant tiny lights transform the performers and floats into fanciful scenes from Walt Disney film classics to its distinctive soundtrack, "Baroque Hoedown."

Golden State

Grizzly Peak may look like the High Sierra on the outside but its massive concrete-and-steel boulders hide the complex and powerful pump equipment that sends 130,000 gallons of water a minute roaring down the Grizzly River Run (opposite page).

Get a ranger's eye-view of the Golden State land from atop one of the Redwood Creek Challenge Trail's three fire towers (right).

Throughout its history, California's temperate climate, distinctly different topographies, and bountiful resources have attracted a multicultural population of adventurers and entrepreneurs. The Golden State land, with its variety of rustic landscapes and exciting rides and attractions, exemplifies California's rich diversity of land, heritage, and people.

Under the watchful eye of Grizzly Peak, thrill seekers can race down swirling white water on an exhilarating raft ride, brave the challenges faced by state park rangers, or fly over the natural beauty of dense redwood forests and snow-capped mountains. A taste of California is available at unique dining spots that range from the fruits of its fertile valleys and northern wine-making country to the hearty ethnic foods enjoyed along its rocky coastline.

Explore the high desert airfields evoking the early years of the modern aviation era, the romance of a mountain campground, and the history of a land where opportunity is truly "golden."

Condor Flats

Celebrate California's aviation history at Condor Flats, inspired by the world of airplane test pilots from the time when the sound barrier was first broken in the late 1940s. Aircraft memorabilia, weathered airplane hangars, and test equipment are all incorporated into the dusty landscape of this "renewed" high-desert airfield. Shop at the Fly 'N' Buy, view demonstrations of California's important contributions to air travel, or have a meal at the Taste Pilots' Grill, which serves up food for hungry flyboys and girls. Look for the Quonset hut hangar with a replica of the world's first supersonic aircraft, an X-1 jet, bursting through the top.

Soarin' Over California

Fly high above the wonders of California in the most realistic free-flight experience ever created. After ascending 44 feet within an Omnimax dome that completely surrounds their field of vision—over, under, left, and right—guests literally soar over the awesome beauty of Yosemite, glide over a Tahoe ski slope, and race above the desert floor accompanied by six Air Force Thunderbirds. The feel of the wind over the Golden Gate and the sweet scent of orange blossoms and pine trees over the Redwood forests enhances this incredible journey.

Grizzly Peak Recreation Area

Evoking the pristine wilderness and natural beauty of California's state and national parks, Grizzly Peak Recreation Area celebrates the great outdoors amid towering pine trees and rustic scenery. Sheltered under the craggy countenance of Grizzly Peak Mountain, a leisurely walk through this mini-wilderness area is a delight to the senses as trails meander over and around landscapes inspired by the High Sierras.

Grizzly River Run

White-knuckle it down Grizzly River
Run on one of the most sophisticated
white-water rafting rides of its kind.
The wet and wild fun begins in the
shadow of Grizzly Peak as circular
rafts float past towering redwoods
and around an abandoned mining
town before careening over a water-
fall into a wild-water rampage like
no other. Not only do the ride
vehicles drop through slides and
caverns but they also spin as they
fall, ending with a soaking plunge
into an erupting geyser field.

Redwood Creek Challenge Trail

The world of California's park rangers is re-created in a high energy, fun-filled obstacle course set among a trio of ranger fire towers. Adventurous guests can slide down the Hoot-N-Holler Logs, bounce over cargo netting and springy suspension bridges, explore the Tunnel Tree Crawl Thru and Hibernation Hollow, or scale the rocky surface of Cliff Hanger Rock Climb. At the Ahwahnee Camp Circle (below right), where split logs and tree stumps serve as seats, guests enjoy Native-American tribal fables or ghost stories and sing-a-longs around a flickering campfire.

Bountiful Valley Farm

Savor the rich agricultural heritage of California in the shade of avocado, almond, and apple trees and a bower of orange, lemon, and grapefruit groves at Bountiful Valley Farm presented by Caterpillar Inc. Hands-on exhibits educate guests about irrigation techniques, farm machinery, pest control, and the process of getting food from the field to the table. Enjoy fresh fruits, vegetables, salads, or turkey legs at the farmer's market food court next door or relax with a frothy cold drink at Sam Andreas Shakes before visiting the Irrigation Station and its playground of spritzing pipes. Guests can also pick up flowers and decorations at Santa Rosa Seed & Supply for their own gardening needs.

It's Tough To Be A Bug!

This creepy crawly 3-D show finds an appropriate home in the dark underground cave next to Bountiful Valley Farm in A Bug's Land. Join Flik, Hopper, and zillions of wriggling friends from *A Bug's Life* as they come right off the screen and into the theater to give guests a "bug's-eye" view of the perils of insect life. The 3-D adventure movie features an abundance of insects including tarantulas, termites, and the most odoriferous member of the bug world, the "silent but deadly" stinkbug.

The Golden Vine Winery

The world-famous Napa Valley provides inspiration for The Golden Vine Winery, nestled against Grizzly Mountain. Guests can stroll through the vineyards or sample new vintages at on-site wine-tasting sessions. The Mission-style buildings are surrounded by lush terraced vistas in a grapevine-strewn countryside. Dine at the Vineyard Room, where elegant foods and wines are paired with a breathtaking view of the Golden State land, or sit under the trees while enjoying "take-out" items from the Wine Country Market.

Golden Dreams

Created exclusively for Disney's California Adventure Park, *Golden Dreams* is a powerful, moving film honoring the people whose hopes, dreams, and hard work have shaped California. Queen Califia, the mythical spirit of California, narrates the journey, from the first Native Americans, the arrival of Spanish settlers, the Gold Rush era, and the building of the railroads, to the immigration of farm workers, the founding of the movie industry, through the 60s pop culture and the rise of the computer generation.

Pacific Wharf

Inspired by Monterey's Cannery
Row, this waterfront industrial area
recognizes the contributions of the
many diverse cultures that settled
the northern California coastline.
On-site workshops and tours
demonstrate the assembly-line
production of the various foods
produced in these micro-factories.
Walking through the hodgepodge of
wood and brick buildings, guests can
peek into Boudin Bakery to watch
Sourdough Bread being made, see
tortillas roll off the line at Mission
Tortilla Factory (right), and puzzle
over the elaborate fortune cookie-
making machinery at The Lucky
Fortune Cookery.

Pacific Wharf Dining

The diversity of Pacific Wharf's cuisine offers a wide palate of choices for the discriminating gourmand, who can savor their selection on outdoor patios. Enjoy seafood and sandwiches served on oven-fresh Boudin Sourdough French Bread at the Pacific Wharf Café; dim sum, Korean rice dishes, and Chinese egg noodles at The Lucky Fortune Cookery; or specialty tacos wrapped in tortillas from the Mission Tortilla Factory at the Cocina Cucamonga Mexican Grill.

Go "on location" and enjoy the glitzy world of celebrity madness at the Hollywood Pictures Backlot (opposite page).

Enjoy a gourmet coffee or frosty smoothie at Schmoozies!, just one of the many tongue-in-cheek dining options on Hollywood Boulevard (right).

Stargazers get a backstage pass to the glamour of movie-making on the Hollywood Pictures Backlot, where showbiz-themed attractions celebrate America's ongoing love affair with the movies.

Fun and fantasy prevail as you walk down the glittering streets of Hollywood Boulevard lined with the Art Deco and Spanish-style facades that re-create details reminiscent of classic Los Angeles architectural landmarks. Behind the scenes, you can experience hands-on demonstrations of the animator's craft, enjoy 3-D movie merriment, or take in a Broadway-style show. Then ride in a purple limousine for a star's-eye view of movie madness before you dine on the set of your favorite daytime drama.

There's always plenty of lights, cameras, and exciting action on this recreation of the ultimate Hollywood movie studio.

Hollywood Boulevard

Step through the enormous ornate Studio gates and find yourself on a palm-lined boulevard of dreams. Classic Los Angeles architecture was the inspiration for the buildings that line Disney's Hollywood Boulevard and Backlot area, dazzling with stylish Art Deco facades and show biz glamour. Even the street glitters underfoot: just like the real Hollywood Boulevard, the asphalt has a shimmering, star-like sparkle.

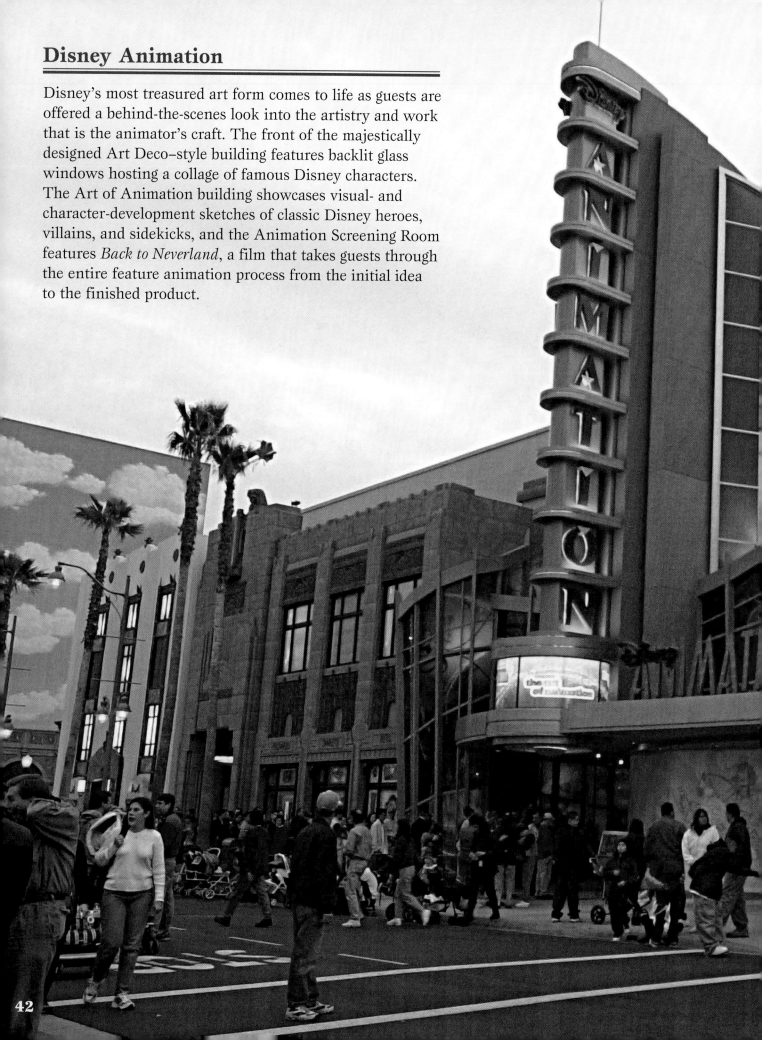

Disney Animation

Disney's most treasured art form comes to life as guests are offered a behind-the-scenes look into the artistry and work that is the animator's craft. The front of the majestically designed Art Deco–style building features backlit glass windows hosting a collage of famous Disney characters. The Art of Animation building showcases visual- and character-development sketches of classic Disney heroes, villains, and sidekicks, and the Animation Screening Room features *Back to Neverland*, a film that takes guests through the entire feature animation process from the initial idea to the finished product.

Inside Animation

After passing through the sixteen giant projection screens in the Courtyard Gallery (above), guests can examine early animation devices in the Sorcerer's Workshop (far left), hear their own voice on a classic Disney clip at Ursula's Grotto, or take a personality survey at Enchanted Books in the Beast's Library (near left), to discover which Disney character they are most like.

Jim Henson's
Muppet*Vision 3D

Set in a lavish showplace reminiscent of the original "Muppet Show" television series, Kermit, Miss Piggy, Fozzie Bear, and a half-dozen other Muppets join together in their first West Coast engagement, intending to enlighten spectators on the art and illusion of three-dimensional film-making. But things don't always go as planned at their fictional studio's FX Research and Development Lab. Evasive action may be necessary when squirt gun sprays, fireworks, and cream pies appear to fly right out of the screen and into the audience in this explosive extravaganza. And no Muppet mayhem would be complete without those consummate hecklers Statler and Waldorf in the balcony.

47

Hyperion Theater

Located at the far end of Hollywood Boulevard is the first Broadway-style enclosed theater ever built in a Disney theme park. Recalling the stylish movie houses of Hollywood's golden age, this ornate, 2,000-seat showplace features high-energy, dazzling song-and-dance musical reviews showcasing live entertainment. The exterior facade is patterned after the Los Angeles Theater, an historic vaudeville performing house. But after guests pass through a garden-patio lobby featuring a wall ornamented with mural panels depicting scenes from life during Hollywood's heyday, the interior is strictly state-of-the-art top-notch technology.

Who Wants To Be A Millionaire - Play It!

This new live-show attraction based on the hit ABC-TV game show *Who Wants To Be A Millionaire* begins when the guest with the fastest finger is chosen from the audience to land in the "hot seat." All contestants play for points, not dollars, on a replica of the famous high-tech *Who Wants To Be A Millionaire* set, complete with its dramatic lighting. Players still have three lifelines for help, but when the guests "phone a friend," the call will go to a complete stranger passing by outside the theater.

ABC Soap Opera Bistro

Enjoy delectable dining at the Llanview Country Club and Stables from *One Life to Live*, Adam Chandler's mansion from *All My Children*, The Docks of *Port Charles*, or dish the dirt at Kelly's Diner, Luke's, or the nurses' station from *General Hospital* at this first-of-its kind restaurant that takes guests onto the sets of their favorite ABC soaps. The waitstaff will also share some exciting previews with you as you enjoy the fun and food. Guests can view a display of actual wardrobe, jewelry, and props from their favorite shows, and merchandise from both the shows and the restaurant are on sale at the adjacent ABC SoapLink.

Superstar Limo

Take a madcap glitzy ride through the star-studded streets of Los Angeles where guests become the most sought-after stars ever to hit the big time. After boarding a purple limousine, you receive a frantic call on the video cell phone—it's Swifty LaRue, your slick Hollywood agent, telling you to rush to a big movie premiere! Along the way you'll zoom past the famous landmarks of Rodeo Drive and Sunset Strip, encounter a Malibu mudslide, and cruise through the affluent neighborhoods of Beverly Hills and Bel Air as you careen towards a happy ending as Hollywood's newest star.

Paradise Pier

The sparkling lights and carnival colors of the Sun Wheel and Maliboomer, encircled by the California Screamin' roller coaster, reflect the high energy and excitement of Paradise Pier at night (opposite page).

Get a between-the-ears view as you circle the Mickey Mouse icon during the California Screamin' roller coaster ride (right).

Fun in the Sun for Everyone!

Fun seekers of all ages will enjoy the high-energy seaside sizzle at Paradise Pier, inspired by the beachfront amusement parks that lined the California coastline in years past. Nostalgic boardwalk attractions combine with state-of-the-art technology for nonstop thrills and chills. Speed along a roller coaster that features a 360-degree loop around a silhouette of Mickey Mouse's head or shoot up a towering rendition of a strength-testing game, then ride a beautifully sculpted dolphin or flying fish on an aquatic themed carousel. You can even swing around the inside of a huge California orange to the sound of buzzing bumblebees.

Try your luck at the festive midway booths that line the boardwalk by pitching, fishing, or dunking your way to a prize, as the scent of cotton candy swirls in the air. Then end the day with a delicious meal on the outdoor patio of a premier family restaurant.

Night Lights

Whimsical designs and seaside ornamentations add a delightful element to the attractions of Paradise Pier all day long but at night, the circles, spheres, and towers of the attractions glow with a giddy excitement. Thousands of twinkling lights and visual effects transform the area into a dazzling display of brilliant colors. The magic is mirrored in the reflecting waters of Paradise Bay.

California Screamin'™

At the southernmost end of Paradise Pier, the California Screamin' roller coaster provides high-intensity thrills and white-knuckle chills when it literally catapults guests from 0 to 55mph in a 5-second incline before sending its passengers over, under, and around a 6,000-foot steel-reinforced track. Though its "wooden" look is nostalgic, its technology is strictly 21ˢᵗ century. Every twist and turn is synchronized to a pounding soundtrack as riders race over the midway games area and whip around the crashing waves of the Paradise Pier Bay. "Scream tunnels" set in various locations help muffle the shrieks as guests climb up and drop down, before the ride climaxes with a 360-degree loop-the-loop around the outline of a giant stylized Mickey Mouse head.

Sun Wheel

Within its 150-foot diameter, the celestial-faced Sun Wheel features a ride-within-a-ride like no other. Passengers can view the entire park from across the four-acre bay as they ride in this beautifully designed Wonder Wheel, one of only three spinning wheels that exist in the world. Sixteen of the wheel's 24 six-person gondolas actually slide in, out, and around on tracks laced within the diameter of the outer wheel but, fortunately, the gondolas are color-coded to warn those who prefer a milder ride. Its friendly, beaming sun face and blinking lights transform the wheel into kinetic sculpture and make it one of the park's most recognizable icons.

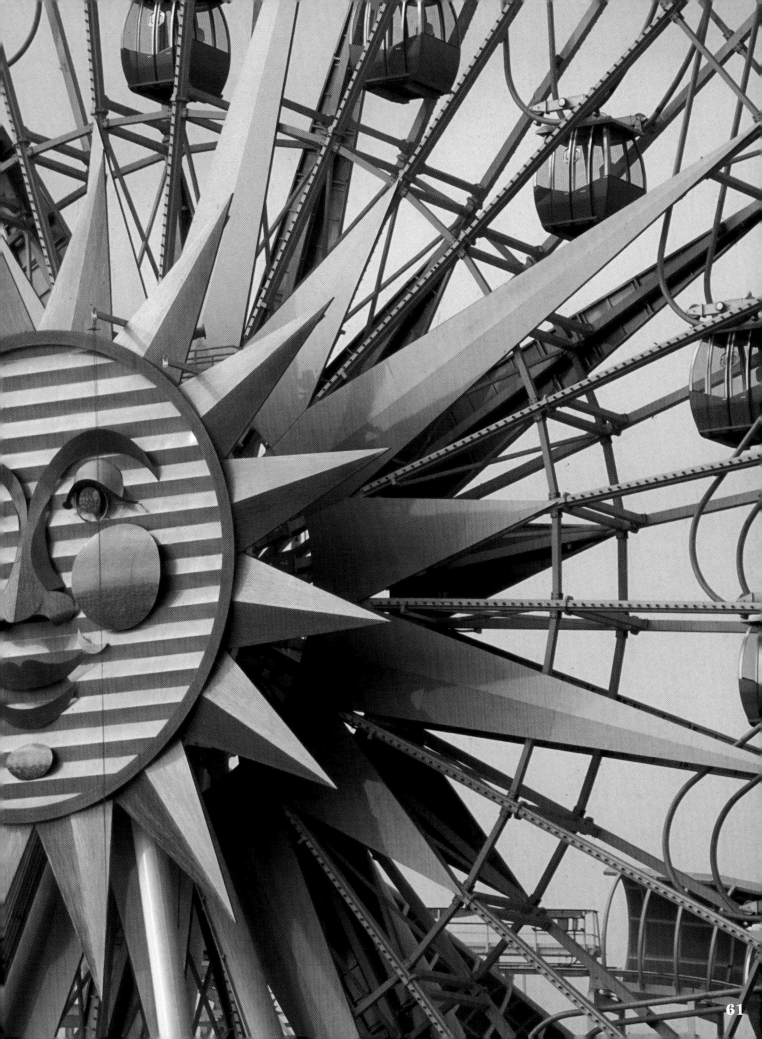

Maliboomer

Swing the mallet, ring the bell, win a prize! The Maliboomer takes the strength-testing games of years past a giant step further as it catapults guests skyward 180 feet in only two seconds in its jet-lift carriages. Then, bungee-like, passengers slowly bounce back to earth—and catch their breath—on one of its three towers. At night, glowing yellow, blue, pink, and purple lights add to the dizzying fun.

Orange Stinger

This giant swing ride has lots of "a-peel" as guests ride in faster and faster circles inside the sphere of a half-peeled California orange. As passengers buzz along, picking up speed, a lone droning bee on the soundtrack is joined by others until the entire citrus-scented interior reverberates with the sound of a swarming hive.

Jumpin' Jellyfish

Young thrill seekers sit in brightly colored jellyfish-shaped vehicles as they rise to the top of a 50-foot tower in this kiddie version of a vertical parachute ride. Then the bell of the jellyfish unfolds and its tentacles fly in the wind as passengers float slowly back to the ground-level kelp bed.

King Triton's Carousel

Carousels are the heart of any board-walk, and this one is quintessentially Californian. Riders are carried round and round on bejeweled, hand-painted ocean creatures that include sea lions, otters, dolphins, whales, and Garibaldi fish (the state saltwater fish of California) while a classic band organ plays 1960s-style surf songs.

Mulholland Madness

Described as "the world's smallest, slowest, most terrifying roller coaster," Mulholland Madness sends guests through a California map book cover onto a wacky trip over the California freeway system from the Hollywood Hills to Malibu. Each four-seater car parodies a classic West Coast vehicle, including a highway patrol car, a woody, or a hot rod blazing with painted flames, as it winds along a billboard-lined course, pivoting sharply around a maze of tight curves through a landscape of sight gags and freeway frolics. Dinosaur Jack and his Sunglass Shack (above) watches over the fun.

Golden Zephyr

Climb aboard a 12-passenger rocket-ship for a nostalgic and exhilarating swing-ride. Six steel-and-chrome futuristic spaceships are suspended by cables from a rotating 85-foot tower as they spin their passengers in a wide arc over Paradise Pier Bay. A gleaming, sun-lit spectacular attraction by day, the Golden Zephyr is illuminated by sparkling rim lights and the Paradise Pier logo at night.

Games of the Boardwalk

Classic seaside amusement is brought into the present day as the Boardwalk leads guests onto the Midway and its exciting games of skill and chance. Amid the barker's cry of "Step Right Up—Win a Prize!" test your luck at the Dolphin Derby, angle for magnet "fish" at the New Haul Fishery, or shoot hoops at the Shore Shot. Sample the fusion food at Malibu-Ritos, where Malibu meets Mexico, Catch a Flave of soft-serve ice cream with a twist of fruit in the center, or check out your reflection in mirrors that warp and stretch at Sideshow Shirts. The aroma of cotton candy fills the air and a sideshow sense of play prevails as the California Screamin' roller coaster rattles above the fun.

Avalon Cove

Located at the edge of Paradise Pier Bay, Avalon Cove offers a fanciful setting for family dining, complemented by an outstanding view of Paradise Pier. The two-story structure, with its whimsical sand castle design topped by glittering conical towers, hosts seaside supping with some of Disney's best-loved characters. Guests can enjoy their meal in the "undersea" area, complete with seashell-shaped booths, or outdoors on the patio.

DISNEYLAND RESORT HOTELS AND DOWNTOWN DISNEY

Family-friendly themed resorts, world-class shopping, and high-energy entertainment complement the fun at the hotels and  marketplaces of the Disneyland Resort.

Centrally located between the Disneyland Resort theme parks and hotels, Downtown Disney offers an enticing public esplanade of themed dining, sophisticated shopping, and family-oriented entertainment. **DOWNTOWN DISNEY**

The best word to describe a stay at a Disneyland Resort hotel is magical. The traditional Disneyland Hotel and Disney's Paradise Pier Hotel cast their own spell of enchantment with endless opportunities for great dining, invigorating recreation,  and souvenir shopping. Disney's Grand Californian Hotel provides a spectacular view of the excitement at Disney's California Adventure Park.

Disney's Grand Californian Hotel©

The first-ever hotel within a Disney theme-park captures the romantic style of the California Arts and Crafts era in its distinct architecture, luxurious rooms, and its creative and charming recreational amenities. In addition to a cozy hearth-side lounge, sequoia-lined courtyard, and character breakfasts, saunas and massages are offered at Eureka Springs, a state-of-the-art health club. Many of its 751 rooms have balconies with views of either Disney's California Adventure Park or Downtown Disney.

Arts and Crafts

Disney's Grand Californian Hotel reflects the Arts and Crafts design movement of the late nineteenth and early twentieth centuries with its elegant, naturalistic beauty, layered with the unique warmth and color of California. The airy six-story main lobby (left), with massive wooden trusses, inlaid stained-glass railings, and tile-inset wood paneling, creates a feeling of standing in a light-filled forest. The carpet complements the setting with a lush field of native flora such as California poppies and lilies, bordered by a dramatically colored perimeter composed of fourteen different granites and marbles. Bronze and glass light fixtures and terra cotta images of dancing bears provide decorative accents.

Grand Californian Dining

The Storyteller's Cafe (above), a roomy family restaurant featuring American contemporary cuisine, conveys the magic of storytelling in its playful decorations. A large mural depicts a child reading a book, while paintings portraying stories from California literature line the walls. Early in the morning, Chip 'n' Dale visit during breakfast. At the Napa Rose (right), the finest dishes from the state's bountiful farms, dairies, and seacoasts are served in an elegant setting that celebrates the wine country. The restaurant also offers a selection of more than 200 wines to taste while enjoying a stunning view of Grizzly Peak through floor-to-ceiling windows.

Disney's Paradise Pier Hotel®

Comfortable and casual, Disney's Paradise Pier Hotel offers relaxation, family dining, and spectacular views of Disney's California Adventure Park. Guests can have breakfast with Minnie and friends (top, far right), as well as soak in a soothing spa, take a dip in the rooftop pool, or work out at Team Mickey's.

Disneyland Hotel®

Goofy greets guests arriving at the Disneyland Hotel, located on Magic Way. The hotel features fun restaurants and premier shopping, plus three swimming pools and a sandy beach. The magical Never Land pool, based on the animated classic *Peter Pan*, showcases Captain Hook's pirate ship, and Skull Rock, where adventurous guests can ride down a 110 foot-long water slide. Hook's Pointe and Wine Cellar offers mesquite-grilled specialities in a contemporary setting. At night, the resort comes alive with exciting entertainment including Fantasy Waters, a display of colorful lights and water fountains choreographed to a medley of Disney tunes, and live music at the host bar.

Downtown Disney®

Downtown Disney District provides high energy entertainment, dining, and shopping, set in a luxuriant landscape filled with nearly 200 species of plants amid its eclectic architecture. Linking the old park with the new, the Imagineers who created Downtown Disney wedded Old World ambience with contemporary American energy. At the center of Paradise Plaza (above), a fountain shaped like a California poppy (the state flower) adds coolness to the hot live music area.

Ralph Brennan's Jazz Kitchen

Let the good times roll at Ralph Brennan's Jazz Kitchen! Whether you're dining in the courtyard, or on the upstairs jazz balcony, this taste of the Big Easy offers the best of New Orleans cuisine, the high energy kick of Dixieland, and a non-stop party atmosphere.

AMC® Theaters

There's wall-to-wall entertainment at the 12-screen AMC Theater. Inspired by the golden days of Hollywood, each theater offers love seat-style stadium seating, THX Surround Sound, and state-of-the-art amenities including the signature AMC cupholder, and a great choice of films and viewing times.

Catal Restaurant and Uva Bar

Catal Restaurant offers an exotic menu from the world-renowned founder of the Patina restaurants, with dishes that range from hearty soups and salads to fresh seafood and grilled delights from around the globe. The indoor/outdoor UVA Bar recalls the romance of California's picturesque wine region, offering guests a vast menu of tapas, snack-sized dishes featuring an array of flavors and ingredients from the Mediterranean rim.

Rainforest Cafe®

In lush tropical surroundings, guests feast on tasty dishes from Mexico, Asia, and the Caribbean. This 600-seat restaurant, located near the entrance of Downtown Disney, offers a wild place to shop and eat, complete with exotic animals and the occasional thunderstorm.

House of Blues®

Everyone wants to get the Blues! The best of Delta-inspired southern-style cooking and California regional cuisine is served from an open-air kitchen, while next door the specialties include rock, jazz, gospel and, of course, the blues.

Y Arriba Y Arriba

It's a nonstop sizzling showcase of Latin culture at Y Arriba, Y Arriba, a unique tapas-teatro. Mariachi and flamenco dancers, strolling musicians, and an in-house cast complement the emerging and star performers who appear at the teatro while patrons sample a wide-ranging selection of Latin delicacies.

ESPN Zone®

At this premier sports dining and entertainment complex, guests can challenge themselves on the Sports Arena's interactive games, view the latest sporting events on more than 175 video monitors (including some in the bathrooms!), or watch their favorite athletes being interviewed at the ESPN Zone's studio.

World of Disney™

Second in size only to its sister store at the Walt Disney World Resort, this shopping palace offers favorite Disney character merchandise in a colorful environment that includes a 20-foot high wall featuring more than 15,000 plush character toys, murals that carry the motif of "travel" with famous Disney friends portrayed in adventurous spots around the world, and a giant video screen that plays scenes from classic Disney films. Plus a huge collection of backpacks, books, clothing, collectibles, jewelry, sleepwear, souvenirs, videos, watches, and more.

A Journey Through Disneyland Park

A journey through Disneyland Park is a trip like no other.

 Here you can literally walk in Walt's footsteps, revisit adventures and attractions from the past, and enjoy an ever-changing range of new experiences. For  first-time guests, Disneyland Park is a big, shiny gift just waiting to be unwrapped, explored, and enjoyed at every turn. For returning guests, it is like visiting a dear friend or attending a family reunion. Disneyland is a kaleidoscope of memories made anew. So put on your Mickey

 Mouse ears, wind-up your camera, and get ready to explore "The Happiest Place on Earth!"

Dusk illuminates the stately architecture of Disneyland City Hall in Town Square, a place to meet, greet, or rest your feet after an exhilarating day. The eucalyptus trees behind City Hall were planted around 1910, making them a truly authentic piece of Main Street (opposite page).

The skyline of Main Street shimmers as its pin lights create a romantic contrast against the sunset (right).

Disneyland Park memories begin on Main Street, U.S.A. Time seems to slow amid the smells of freshly baked muffins and candies, the steady clip-clop of the horse-drawn streetcar, and the twinkling pin lights outlining the gingerbread trim of the buildings. Through the years, Main Street has become an unofficial hometown for the many Disneyland guests who have traversed its charming lane, experienced its unique shops, been entertained by its performers, and dined from its delightful menus.

"Here is America from 1890 to 1910, at the crossroads of an era," Walt Disney once commented. "Here the gas lamp is giving way to the electric lamp, and a newcomer, the sputtering 'horseless carriage,' has challenged Old Dobbin for the streetcar right-of-way." Inspired by Walt's own hometown of Marceline, Missouri, Main Street is the essence of the hometown America that greeted the dawn of the 20th century.

Town Square

Town Square is the civic center of this beguiling Victorian "hometown." The famed Disneyland Band gives daily concerts in the square, and would-be firefighters of the future can enjoy a playful trip into the past on Disneyland Fire Department No. 105. Above the firehouse, Walt Disney kept a small apartment for his visits to Disneyland Park. It is still maintained in Victorian-era décor and has remained virtually unchanged since Walt last used it back in the mid-1960s.

Town Square is also the hub of all Main Street transportation. From here guests can travel in style up Main Street in an open-air horse-drawn streetcar, Main Street fire engine (with clanging alarm bell), horseless carriage, or double-decker Omnibus.

BEHIND THE SCENES

Guests strolling down Main Street may notice that the ornate window advertisements above the attractions, stores, and restaurants add a nice, decorative element, accentuating the turn-of-the-century theme. But only insiders are likely to know that most of the windows also serve a dual purpose of honoring Disneyland cast members, Imagineers, and artists who have left an indelible mark on Disneyland Park. A good example is a window above the Emporium that reads: Elias Disney, Contractor, Est. 1895. Walt Disney's father was, in fact, a general contractor in the Midwest, who opened his contracting office in Chicago in 1895.

Disneyland Railroad

At the Main Street Station (right) guests can board one of the four authentic steam trains of the Disneyland Railroad for a grand circle tour of the park. The *C. K. Holliday* and *E. P. Ripley* were built from scratch at The Walt Disney Studio in Burbank, California, prior to the opening of Disneyland Park. The *Fred G. Gurley* was built in 1894 and was used in Louisiana to haul sugar cane. The *Ernest S. Marsh* was built in 1925 and was used at a lumber mill in New England. The four engines were named after the founders and executives of the Santa Fe Railroad.

During the trip around the park, guests travel along the rim of the Grand Canyon (below top) and journey through the incredible Primeval World (below bottom).

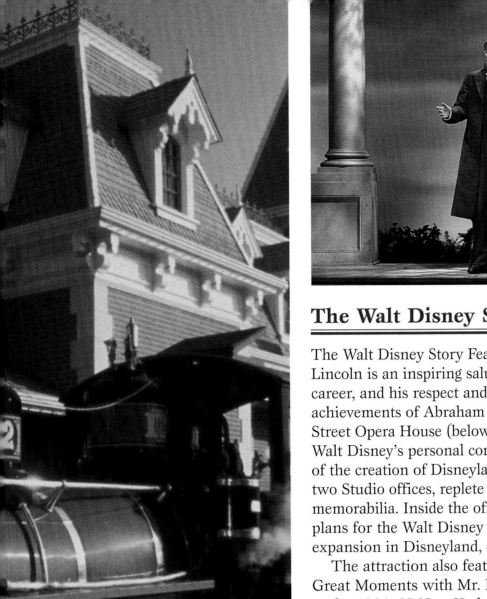

The Walt Disney Story

The Walt Disney Story Featuring Great Moments with Mr. Lincoln is an inspiring salute to Walt Disney, his pioneering career, and his respect and admiration for the wisdom and achievements of Abraham Lincoln. Located in the Main Street Opera House (below), the show features a display of Walt Disney's personal correspondence, early archival photos of the creation of Disneyland Park, and replicas of Disney's two Studio offices, replete with authentic décor and personal memorabilia. Inside the office displays, guests can see early plans for the Walt Disney World Resort and ideas for future expansion in Disneyland, circa 1966.

The attraction also features an updated presentation of Great Moments with Mr. Lincoln, which first premiered at the 1964–65 New York World's Fair before coming to Disneyland. A more lived-in Honest Abe now refers to handheld notes and takes a seat after guests hear his speech delivered through surround sound-enhanced head phones.

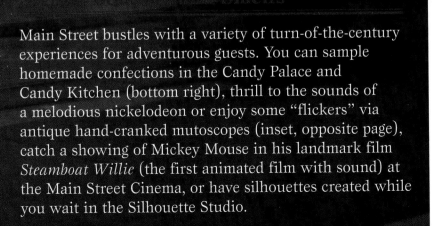

Main Street bustles with a variety of turn-of-the-century experiences for adventurous guests. You can sample homemade confections in the Candy Palace and Candy Kitchen (bottom right), thrill to the sounds of a melodious nickelodeon or enjoy some "flickers" via antique hand-cranked mutoscopes (inset, opposite page), catch a showing of Mickey Mouse in his landmark film *Steamboat Willie* (the first animated film with sound) at the Main Street Cinema, or have silhouettes created while you wait in the Silhouette Studio.

The Miracle of the Hub

One of the most innovative design elements of Disneyland Park can be found at the end of Main Street, U.S.A. The park was planned with a central point of orientation—a "Plaza Hub"— where the entrances to all the "lands" converge, giving guests a convenient center from which to enter and exit. Within the park-like setting of the Plaza Hub, guests can sit among the colorful flowers and plot their next course through Disneyland Park or simply watch the world go by.

"Partners," a bronze statue of Walt Disney and Mickey Mouse, was unveiled in the center of the Plaza Hub in 1993. Set amidst a beautiful and ever-changing array of flowers, the impressive sculpture captures Walt and Mickey as they gaze down Main Street, U.S.A. The perfect focal point of the Hub—celebrating at one and the same time Disneyland's creator and its most famous icon—"Partners" has become one of the most photographed locations in the park.

Adventureland®

Guests encounter the wrath of the deity Mara inside the Temple of the Forbidden Eye as their transport vehicle speeds through the sinister catacombs and dangerous caverns of the Indiana Jones™ Adventure (opposite page).

Cool tranquil pools and cascading waterfalls are an escape from the tropical heat of Adventureland for some playful elephants along the waterways of the Jungle Cruise (right).

As brave Disneyland Park guests enter Adventureland their senses are stirred by the sights of intense jungle foliage, the harrowing sounds of not-too-distant wild animals, and the aromas of tropical blossoms. In this remarkable realm of adventure and exploration, guests experience an amazing amalgam of many of the world's far-off places and uncharted regions.

One quick turn can lead you to the hot sands of the Middle East (Aladdin's Oasis), the tropic splendor of Polynesia (Walt Disney's Enchanted Tiki Room), the vastness of Africa (Tarzan's Treehouse®), the exotic rivers of the world (Jungle Cruise), or the archeological ruins of India (Indiana Jones™ Adventure).

"Here is adventure," Walt Disney commented. "Here is romance. Here is mystery. Tropical rivers . . . silently flowing into the unknown. The unbelievable splendor of exotic flowers . . . the eerie sound of the jungle . . . with eyes that are always watching. This is Adventureland."

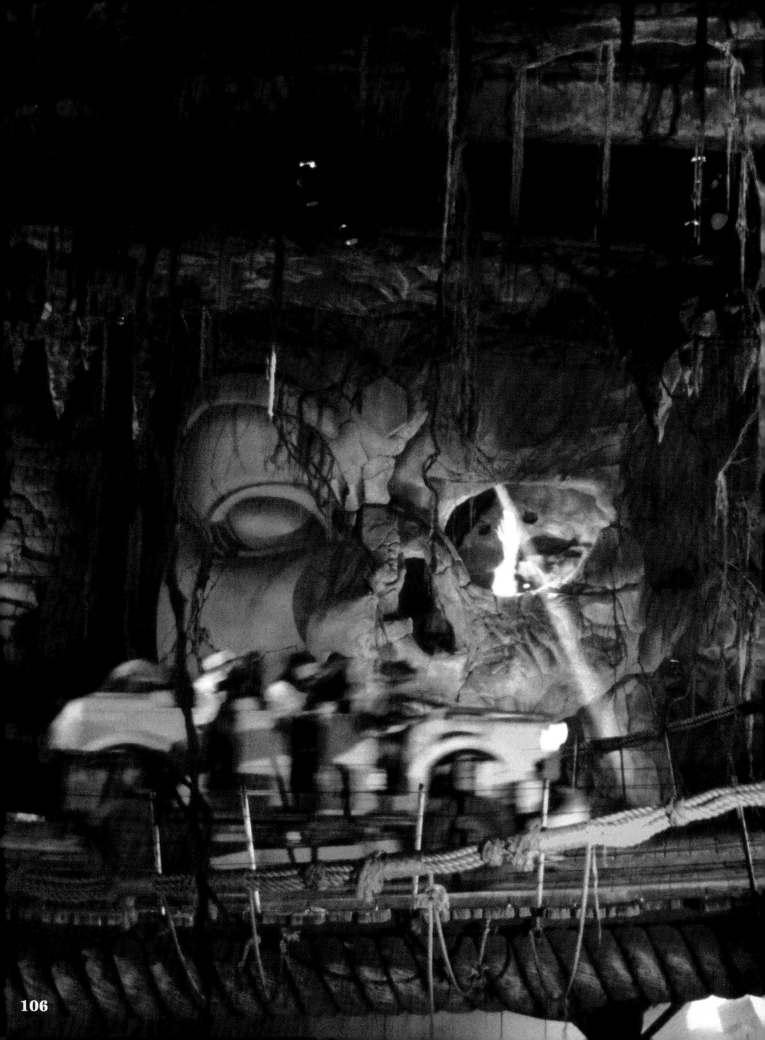

Indiana Jones™ and the Temple of the Forbidden Eye

Join Professor Jones deep inside India for the Indiana Jones™ Adventure. It's 1935 and discovery awaits in the Temple of the Forbidden Eye. Guests board well-worn troop transports that send them into a subterranean world where they have an unfortunate encounter with the mysterious temple deity Mara in the great Chamber of Destiny. Forced to flee, guests narrowly escape a collapsing bridge, booby traps, giant snakes, thousands of rats, and the prospect of being crushed by a 5-ton boulder. The Indiana Jones™ Adventure is one of the most technologically advanced attractions in any of the Disney theme parks. Each of the 16 troop transport vehicles has its own onboard ride control and audio system, allowing it to create nearly 160,000 journey combinations.

Jungle Cruise

One of the original attractions from the opening day of Disneyland Park, the Jungle Cruise has hosted millions of would-be explorers aboard its dangerous (if you count the bad puns) excursions into the jungle. The Jungle Cruise replicates the environs of many of the world's most exotic rivers: the Irrawaddy River of Burma, Cambodia's Mekong, the Nile, the Congo River in Africa, and the Rapids of Kilimanjaro.

From the safety of their launches, guests can witness the gathering of animals on the African Veldt and experience the amazing sight of the "backside" of water under Schweitzer Falls (named after that famous explorer Dr. Albert Falls). They may even catch a rare glimpse of the "Lost Safari," an unfortunate group of adventurers who always seem to be seen in the company of an angry rhino.

Enchanted Tiki Room

At the entrance to Adventureland, Walt Disney's Enchanted Tiki Room entertains guests with an irreverent presentation in which "the birdies sing and the flowers croon." The macaw hosts of the show—José, Michael, Fritz, and Pierre—have welcomed hundreds of thousands of guests into this special "world of joyous songs and wondrous miracles." During the show over 225 birds, flowers, and tikis delight the audience with a rousing rendition of "Let's All Sing Like the Birdies Sing."

BEHIND THE SCENES

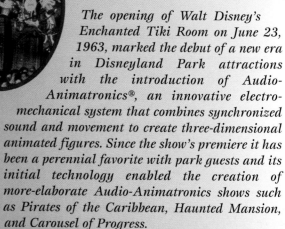

The opening of Walt Disney's Enchanted Tiki Room on June 23, 1963, marked the debut of a new era in Disneyland Park attractions with the introduction of Audio-Animatronics®, an innovative electro-mechanical system that combines synchronized sound and movement to create three-dimensional animated figures. Since the show's premiere it has been a perennial favorite with park guests and its initial technology enabled the creation of more-elaborate Audio-Animatronics shows such as Pirates of the Caribbean, Haunted Mansion, and Carousel of Progress.

Tarzan's Treehouse®

Tarzan's Treehouse® celebrates the high-flying escapades of the "Lord of the Apes" 70 feet above Adventureland. Based on Disney's hit animated film *Tarzan*®, this new climb-through adventure allows guests to meet Tarzan, Jane, and the ferocious tiger Sabor. The tree itself is a very rare "species" known as a *Disneydendron semperflorens grandis* (meaning "large ever-blooming Disney tree"). It weighs 150 tons, features 450 branches and 6,000 leaves, and is anchored by massive "roots" reaching 42 feet into the ground.

Behind the shingled, rough-hewn facades of this wilderness outpost, "pioneering" guests can purchase Western-themed hats, jewelry, crafts, foods, and other supplies (opposite page).

Enjoy a relaxing ride beneath the 84-foot mainmast of the *Columbia* Sailing Ship as it circumnavigates the Rivers of America (right).

T he breathtaking sight of the gleaming white *Mark Twain* Riverboat and the imposing gallantry of the *Columbia* Sailing Ship approaching the dock beckons guests into Frontierland, a robust panorama of America's pioneer past. As you pass through the stockade entrance you are surrounded by an amalgam of sights and sounds that authentically conjures up images from America's mid-nineteenth-century western expansion, from the bustling riverfronts of the Mississippi and Missouri rivers to the raucous and dusty desert southwest.

"Here we experience the story of our country's past . . . the colorful drama of Frontier America in the exciting days of the covered wagon and the stagecoach . . . the advent of the railroad . . . and the romantic riverboat," Walt Disney once commented. "Frontierland is a tribute to the faith, courage, and ingenuity of the pioneers who blazed the trails across America."

Frontierland®

The heroes, legends, and tall tales of the American West live on in Frontierland. Here Davy Crockett is still "King," Tom Sawyer eludes danger inside Injun Joe's Cave, Pecos Bill is still "the toughest critter west of the Alamo," and the ghostly legend of Big Thunder Mountain still haunts wary listeners.

Along the clapboard walkways, dusty trails, and rivers of Frontierland, guests relive our rich pioneer heritage, including the charm of Old Mexico in Zocalo Park, an authentic encampment of Plains Indians along the riverbank, and the rollicking entertainment inside the Golden Horseshoe saloon.

115

Rivers of America

The Rivers of America provides a variety of ways for would-be pioneers of all ages to explore the wilderness outposts of Frontierland. The dazzling white *Mark Twain* Riverboat carries guests upriver in southern elegance. When it opened in 1955, the *Mark Twain* was the first paddle wheeler built in the United States in half a century. The 10-gun *Columbia* Sailing Ship lets passengers relive life aboard an authentic replica of the first American ship to sail around the world. The *Columbia* was the first three-masted windjammer built in the United States in more than 100 years when it opened in 1958. Guests can get a close-up look of river life as they ride the backwaters of the Rivers of America.

Tom Sawyer Island

Walt Disney, who spent his early childhood in Missouri, personally oversaw the design of Tom Sawyer Island. Filled with such playful locales as Teeter-Totter Rock, Smuggler's Cove, and Tom and Huck's Treehouse, the island is a cool, shady oasis of adventure. Young modern-day Tom Sawyers, Huck Finns, and Becky Thatchers still find fun on a rollicking barrel bridge or in the authenticity of log-hewn Fort Wilderness.

Big Thunder Mountain Railroad

Big Thunder Mountain Railroad— "the wildest ride in the wilderness!" —whisks brave guests back to the Gold Rush era aboard runaway mine trains that race around towering buttes, dive into dangerous gulches, and plunge deep into caverns filled with bats and phosphorescent pools. The reckless trains careen past raging waterfalls, splash through still waters, and finally encounter a deafening earthquake from which the mountain gets its name.

Disney Imagineers scouted swap meets, auctions, ghost towns, and abandoned mines throughout the western United States for items to incorporate into the theming of the first incarnation of Big Thunder Mountain Railroad. The attraction's authentic mining props include a 1,200-pound cogwheel used to break down ore, a hand-powered drill press, and a 10-foot-tall 1880 mill stamp.

Fantasmic!

In 1992 a new tradition in Disneyland Park nighttime entertainment made its debut—Fantasmic! Easily one of the most complex and technically advanced shows ever presented at a Disney theme park, this hugely popular evening extravaganza features a battle of good and evil inside Mickey Mouse's fanciful imagination.

Statistics:

• 12,000 guests can view the show along the shores of the Rivers of America in Frontierland.

• More than 100 cast and crew members are needed to stage one presentation of the show.

• 341 costumes are necessary in order to present the show seven nights a week.

• Three 30-foot-tall by 50-foot-wide mist screens are used in the show; 70 mm film images are projected onto the screens via projectors stationed on Tom Sawyer's Island.

• The 45-foot-tall Sleeping Beauty Dragon breathes fire, setting the river aflame.

123

The holidays bring a special glow and glitter to the ornate balconies of New Orleans Square (opposite page).

Daylight shines brightly on this bend of the river, revealing intricate architectural details and providing a natural spotlight for the many flowers that grace New Orleans Square (right).

Here is the Paris of the American frontier: the Crescent City of New Orleans as it was 150 years ago. Within its sheltered courtyards and winding streets, grace and charm mingle comfortably with the irreverent sounds of Dixieland jazz. In this romantic yet exhilarating setting guests are immersed in the sights and sounds reminiscent of The Big Easy. The aromas of chicory and freshly baked fritters fill the air while the Louisiana state flag flies proudly overhead and the billowing white sails of a mighty galleon can be seen in the distance beyond the city.

New Orleans Square was added to Disneyland Park in 1966. It was the first new "land" to be added to the park since its opening a decade before. From blossoming magnolia trees to intricate hand-painted murals, tiles, and mirrors, to authentic gas lamps and signage, the Disney Imagineers spared no detail in creating a port of elegance and adventure on this particular bend of the river.

Cajun Charm

Under the ornate wrought-iron balconies of New Orleans Square are found some of the most distinctive restaurants and shops in all of Disneyland Park. Fine crystal and antique estate jewelry, hand-decorated parasols, rare high-end collectibles, and authentic Creole and Cajun spices and sauces can be found behind its many French doors. At Café Orleans, the Royal Street Veranda, or the French Market, appetites can be satisfied with such temptations as spicy gumbo, sweet mint juleps, and mouth-watering fried chicken.

"Set sail with the wildest crew that ever sacked the Spanish Main" aboard the beloved high-seas adventure Pirates of the Caribbean. This classic Disneyland Park attraction warns guests that "Dead Men Tell No Tales," but that doesn't dissuade its fun-loving cast of buccaneers from plundering a seaport village in search of treasure and unanimously proclaiming "Yo-Ho (A Pirate's Life for Me)!" From the mysterious grottos of Davy Jones's Locker to the rambunctious antics of scalawags at play, Pirates of the Caribbean provides a memorable adventure for seafarers of all ages. With over 125 lifelike Audio-Animatronics characters, Pirates of the Caribbean at Disneyland is one of the most elaborate of all Disney theme park attractions.

The Haunted Mansion

"Welcome foolish mortals to the Haunted Mansion," home to 999 frightfully funny ghosts and happy haunts—but there is always room for one more! All the spirits are "just dying to meet you" as you tour this stately antebellum mansion in your own private "Doom Buggy." Beware of hitchhiking ghosts—they just may try to follow you home! The Haunted Mansion was in development for more than 10 years until its opening in 1969. The building exterior was actually completed in 1963, tantalizing guests for the next six years.

The organ located in the ballroom of the Mansion is the same organ played by Captain Nemo in Walt Disney's classic live-action film *20,000 Leagues Under the Sea*.

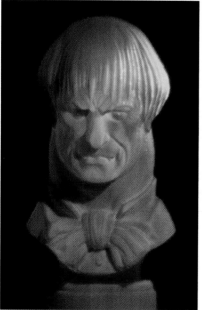 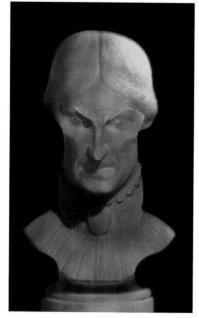

Critter Country®

Intricate woodcarvings of Critter Country's signature trio—Brer Fox, Brer Bear, and Brer Rabbit—grace the shady queue area of Splash Mountain (opposite page).

Guests encounter a rustic signpost at the entrance to Critter Country that perfectly evokes its charm and hospitality (right).

Every day is a "Zip-a-Dee-Doo-Dah" kind of day in Critter Country, a little world of shady trees and cool streams tucked away in a quiet corner of the backwoods of Disneyland Park. Nestled amid a forest of Aleppo, Canary Island, Monterey, and Italian stone pines, along with coast redwood, locusts, white birch, and evergreen elms, Critter Country is the perfect setting for long lazy afternoons and an opportunity to simply delight in the down-home country atmosphere. Keen eyes might spot wily Brer Rabbit outsmarting Brer Fox and Brer Bear atop Chickapin Hill.

Guests with little cubs and hearty appetites can dine along the river's edge at the rustic Hungry Bear Restaurant. And at the Briar Patch, under the looming shadow of Splash Mountain, guests can find items suitable to decorate any den, cave, or home.

Inspired by Walt Disney's classic film *Song of the South* and the wise fables of Uncle Remus, Splash Mountain is the centerpiece of Critter Country and gives brave guests a chance to follow in the perilous footsteps of wily Brer Rabbit. Search for your "Laughing Place" as you journey through this exciting flume adventure which features five drops, including a hair-raising finale that sends you on a 52 foot, 45 degree-angle, 40 mph plunge into a watery briar patch below.

Cross over the moat and through the archways of Sleeping Beauty Castle to enter "the happiest kingdom of them all"— Fantasyland. Enchanting tales of childhood adapted from Walt Disney's classic animated films come to life in this enduring realm of imagination. You can visit Never Land, soar through the skies with Dumbo, journey with little Alice to Wonderland, and travel the road to Pleasure Island with Pinocchio.

"Here is the world of imagination, hopes and dreams," Walt Disney stated on opening day. "In this timeless land of enchantment, the age of chivalry, magic, and make-believe are reborn—and fairy tales come true. Fantasyland is dedicated to the young and the young-in-heart—to those who believe that when you wish upon a star, your dreams come true."

Fantasyland° Enchantment

Dusk casts a veil of additional magic over this happy land of childhood. The medieval splendor of Sleeping Beauty Castle is complemented by the deep shadows of the mighty snowcapped Matterhorn in the distance. Walt Disney once said that "Fantasy, if it's really convincing, can't become dated, for the simple reason that it represents a flight into a dimension that lies beyond the reach of time . . . and nobody gets any older."

King Arthur Carrousel

Beckoning guests through the archway of Sleeping Beauty Castle is the glittering sight of King Arthur Carrousel. The horses of the carrousel are 90 to 110 years old and are hand-carved and hand-painted classics—no two are exactly alike. The turntable for the carrousel was made around 1875 and came from Canada. Most of the 19th-century horses were hand-carved in Germany.

Sleeping Beauty Castle has stood guard over Fantasyland since 1955. The pinks and the blues of the regal, Bavarian-style castle are a nod to the princess for whom the castle is named. Sharp-eyed guests will notice such details as Walt Disney's family crest above the castle entrance and actual 22-karat gold leafing adorning the spires.

Alice in Wonderland

Don't be late for a very important date! Climb aboard your very own private Caterpillar and journey down the rabbit hole to join Alice in her marvelous adventures in Wonderland. Unique to Disneyland Park, the Alice in Wonderland adventure is filled with such memorable scenes as the Unbirthday Party, Tweedledum and Tweedledee, the Garden of Flowers, the March of the Cards, and a fateful round of croquet with the ever-explosive Queen of Hearts.

Pinocchio's Daring Journey

Pinocchio's Daring Journey premiered in Fantasyland in 1983. Guests are sure to be captivated by the lonely woodcarver Geppetto and his desire to have a real son. Along cobblestone alpine roads, guests follow little Pinocchio and his faithful conscience Jiminy Cricket as they attempt to avoid fateful encounters with the conniving Foulfellow and Gideon, the villainous puppeteer Stromboli, and Monstro the Whale. With the "wishing star" as their guide, guests meet the lovely Blue Fairy and ultimately share in Pinocchio's happy ending.

Casey Jr. Circus Train

Guests aboard the Casey Jr. Circus Train (secure in their various cages, boxcars, and cabooses) will cheer along as Casey proclaims "I think I can, I think I can, I think I can" while he chugs and puffs his way through the hills and valleys of Storybook Land. Casey Jr. Circus Train is based upon the brave little circus train featured in Walt Disney's beloved animated film *Dumbo*.

Storybook Land Canal Boats

Aboard the Storybook Land Canal Boats, guests glide past miniature homes and settings from some of Disney's most adored characters and animated films including Geppetto's Village, the Dwarfs' Diamond Mine, and Aladdin's city of Agrabah. Created at 1/12th scale, the intricately detailed dwellings are complemented by actual living miniature shrubs, flowers, and trees including 150-year-old miniature pine trees.

144

Mad Tea Party

Guests can spin and spin and
spin their cup and saucer in any
direction in the Mad Tea Party,
a life-sized Unbirthday Party.
With colorful Chinese paper
lanterns hanging overhead
and the familiar strains
of the "Unbirthday
Song" in the air, guests
will surely feel as if they
stepped right into
the beloved
storybook or
Disney film
Alice in Wonderland.

Dumbo the Flying Elephant

Soar high over Fantasyland aboard Dumbo the Flying
Elephant, a tribute to the world's most famous flying
pachyderm. A well-known European manufacturer
of circus organs built the attraction's vintage
mechanical band organ. Constructed around 1915,
the organ weighs three-quarters of a ton and
resounds with circus-like music.

Peter Pan's Flight

On Peter Pan's Flight guests pilot their own pirate galleon, sailing through the nursery of the Darling family (the toy alphabet blocks in the nursery spell the word "Disney" from the bottom up), gliding over London, and following Tinker Bell towards the "Second Star to the Right" and straight on to Never Land. Amid twinkling stars, you can look down and spy such Never Land locales as Mermaid Lagoon and Skull Rock. More than half of the approximately 350 miles of fiber optics used throughout Fantasyland appear in Peter Pan's Flight.

Snow White's Scary Adventures

Enter a timeless tale of romance in Snow White's Scary Adventures. The lovable Seven Dwarfs celebrate with a "Silly Song" while the evil Queen disguises herself as an old peddler woman to tempt Snow White with a juicy cursed apple. Although the Queen often can be seen staring out of a window above Snow White's Scary Adventures, everyone lives happily ever after with the arrival of the Prince and love's first kiss.

Mr. Toad's Wild Ride

Madcap adventurer J. Thaddeus Toad welcomes guests inside stately Toad Hall as he test drives his all-new motorcar and takes everyone on a wild ride across the English countryside to "Nowhere in Particular." Along the way guests race, leap, and crash their way through Mr. Toad's trials and tribulations inside one of Fantasyland's most beloved attractions. The coat of arms for J. Thaddeus Toad, featured in the décor of Toad Hall, is emblazoned with the motto *Toadi Acceleratio Semper Absurda* ("Speeding with Toad is always absurd").

Snow White Wishing Well

Site of numerous wedding proposals, the Snow White Wishing Well and Grotto provides a tranquil and romantic setting along the east side of the Sleeping Beauty Castle moat. The marble figures of Snow White and the Seven Dwarfs were a gift to Walt Disney from an Italian sculptor. Sharp-eared guests can hear Snow White's hopeful refrain of "I'm Wishing" echoing in the depths of the well.

Triton Gardens & Ariel's Grotto

Under the shadow of the mighty Matterhorn is Triton Gardens, where fanciful spouts of water dance and leap across the walkway to the delight of guests. Across the way, Ariel poses for pictures with guests in her impressive clamshell setting.

The Sword in the Stone

Little would-be monarchs can follow in the footsteps of young King Arthur as they try to remove the legendary sword Excalibur from its anvil and stone resting-place. With a little help from bumbling Merlin the Wizard, royal hopefuls sometimes successfully budge the sword and become rulers of the realm for the day.

Matterhorn Bobsleds

The Matterhorn Bobsleds had its origin in the 1959 Disney film *The Third Man on the Mountain*. Towering 14 stories above Fantasyland, the snow-capped Matterhorn (a 1/100th scale replica of its Swiss namesake) is the setting for a thrilling race through ominous ice caves and a frightening chance encounter with the Abominable Snowman. Along its icy slopes are thundering waterfalls, alpine forests, and tranquil ponds. The camp of the lost climbing expedition inside the Matterhorn is a tribute to former Walt Disney Company President Frank G. Wells. Prior to his passing in 1994, Wells had climbed the highest mountains on six of the seven continents.

"it's a small world"®

Guests have been captivated by "it's a small world" since its premiere at Disneyland Park in 1966. A salute to the children of the world, this delightful attraction speaks the international language of goodwill. Its impressive exterior, featuring spires and finials covered in 22-karat-gold leafing, playfully represents world landmarks, including France's Eiffel Tower, Italy's Leaning Tower of Pisa, and India's famed Taj Mahal. Aboard their boats, guests journey beyond the Topiary Garden and drift with the tide into "The Happiest Cruise That Ever Sailed."

During the winter, the attraction is transformed into the spectacular "it's a small world" Holiday, in which the holiday traditions of many nations are fancifully displayed and the attraction's famous score is beautifully integrated with such holiday favorites as "Deck the Halls" and "Jingle Bells."

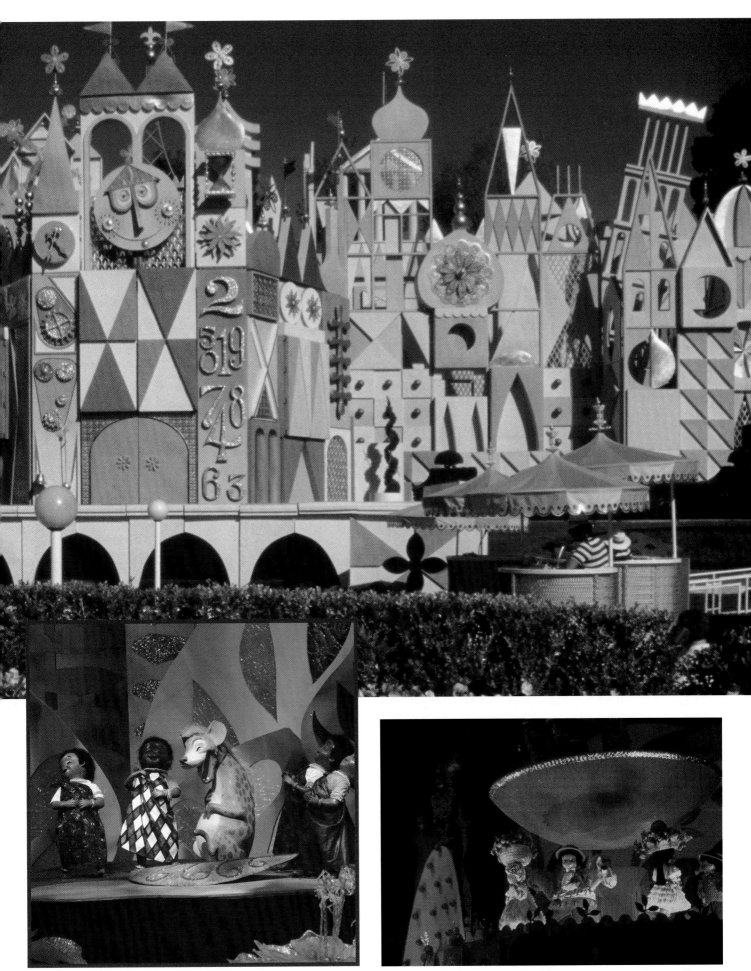

Bursting with color and frenetic energy, Mickey's Toontown is a classic Disney cartoon come to wacky "reel" life. Here in this social hub of "Toon" life, animated stars such as Mickey Mouse, Minnie Mouse, Donald Duck, Goofy, and Roger Rabbit live, work, and play, much to the delight of guests of all ages.

Toontown legend has it that Mickey Mouse founded the three-acre community in the 1930s as a retreat from the bustle of Hollywood. Until its opening in 1993 Toontown was kept secret, the only human allowed inside being Walt Disney. Mickey suggested in the early 1950s that the vacant property to the south be turned into Disneyland Park. Thirty-eight years later, Mickey decided to open Toontown to the public.

Signage leading into Mickey's Toontown announces such organizations as the DAR (Daughters of the Animated Reel), Loyal Knights of the Inkwell, Optimist Intoonational, and the Benevolent and Protective Order of Mouse.

"Toon" in to Toontown

The municipality of Mickey's Toontown is divided into three areas: to the east is the ever active Downtown, in the west are the tranquil environs of Mickey's Neighborhood (home to Mickey, Minnie, Goofy, Donald, and Chip 'n Dale), and Toontown Square is situated in the middle. Mickey's Toontown features some of the most unique architecture in Disneyland Park, with no straight lines, right angles, or conventional methods of construction to be found. Here, mailboxes and manhole covers have personalities (and voices) all their own.

Mickey's House and Meet Mickey

The welcome mat is always out for guests to Mickey's House and Meet Mickey. Inside Mickey's California bungalow home guests can see where Mickey unwinds and view mementos of his famed career.

Through the backyard guests can tour Mickey's Movie Barn Sound Stage where he keeps many of the props from some of his most famous film roles. In the Movie Barn guests can drop in to say hello and pose with Mickey as he works on a new film project.

Minnie's House

Painted in romantic hues of lavender and pink, Minnie's House is situated cozily right next door to Mickey's. Inside Minnie's House guests can play with her computerized vanity, bang out a tune on her pots and pans in the kitchen, or assist her with baking a cake for Mickey. Outside, guests can see her colorful garden and make a wish in her charming wishing well.

Goofy's Bounce House

Inside Goofy's Bounce House kids can literally bounce right off the walls of this wacky home. The floor has just a little extra "cush" and the sofa is so fluffy that it can give little guests a lift! After seeing the instability of the inside, you can easily understand why from the outside Goofy's Bounce House looks like it just might bounce off its foundation.

Gadget's Go-Coaster

Gadget's Go-Coaster, located next to Donald's Boat on Toon Lake, is a high-speed, splash-down contraption for children of all ages. Guests travel in vehicles that resemble oversized acorns. Appearing to be made from large spools, springs, rubber bands, toothbrushes, combs, and other assorted household goods, this little coaster is sure to give guests to Mickey's Toontown a beautiful view along with a few butterflies in their stomachs.

Donald's Boat

Walk across the gangplank over Toon Lake and aboard Donald's Boat—the *Miss Daisy.* Home to the irascible yet lovable Donald Duck, the charming boat gives little sailors the opportunity to clang bells and blow whistles. The *Miss Daisy,* named for Donald's sweetheart, also provides a spectacular view of Mickey's Neighborhood and the Downtown area of Mickey's Toontown.

Chip 'n' Dale's Treehouse

The Toontown home of Chip 'n' Dale, Donald Duck's mischievous chipmunk adversaries, is fittingly nestled in a colorful acorn tree. Here little guests can explore their treetop home.

Jolly Trolley

The bright red and gold-trimmed Jolly Trolley rambles through all of Mickey's Toontown, winding around Roger Rabbit's fountain in Downtown Toontown, traveling into Mickey's Neighborhood, and circling Mickey's fountain. A large gold wind-up key on top of the engine turns as the trolley runs. Disney Imagineers fitted the Jolly Trolley with a Tooned-up chassis and various wheel sizes to produce its ambling, undulating cartoonlike gait.

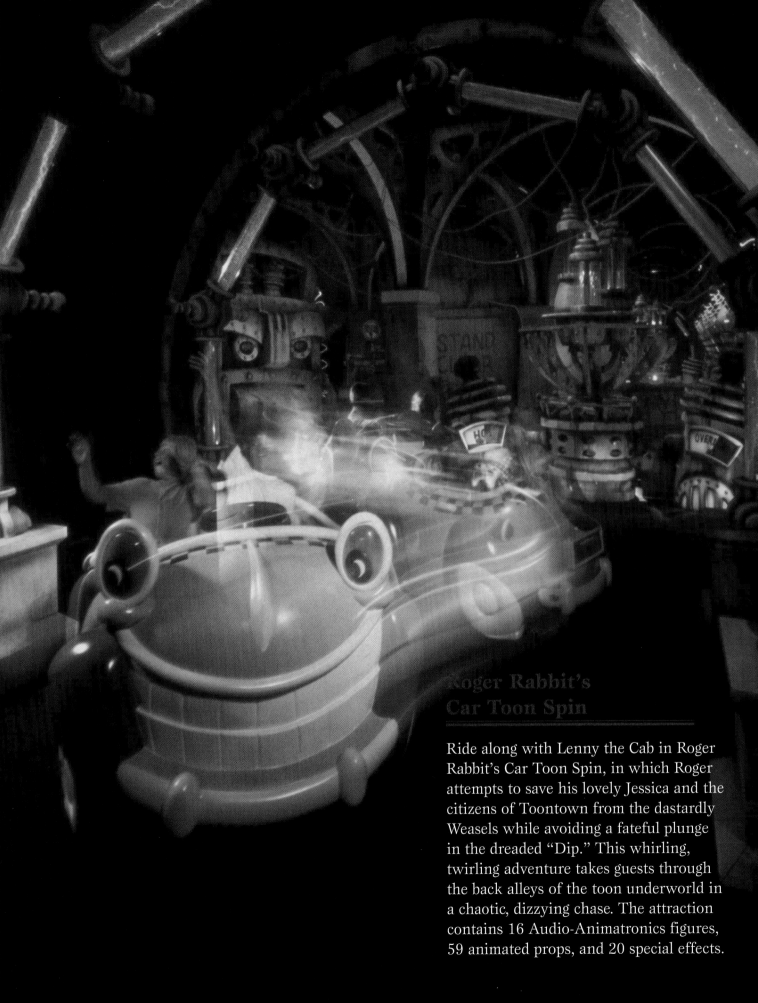

Roger Rabbit's Car Toon Spin

Ride along with Lenny the Cab in Roger Rabbit's Car Toon Spin, in which Roger attempts to save his lovely Jessica and the citizens of Toontown from the dastardly Weasels while avoiding a fateful plunge in the dreaded "Dip." This whirling, twirling adventure takes guests through the back alleys of the toon underworld in a chaotic, dizzying chase. The attraction contains 16 Audio-Animatronics figures, 59 animated props, and 20 special effects.

Tomorrowland ®

The glowing spires of Space Mountain light up the night sky as the Observatron spins in dizzying rainbow spirals above Tomorrowland (opposite page).

The towering Astro Orbiter stands as a welcoming beacon in Tomorrowland (right).

As guests cross over into Tomorrowland, they embark on an exciting journey into "Imagination and Beyond." This intriguing realm of imagination, discovery, and wonder was inspired by such classic futurists as Jules Verne, H. G. Wells, and Leonardo da Vinci, along with modern visionaries like George Lucas. In 1955, when the original Tomorrowland opened, Walt Disney described it as "A vista into a world of wondrous ideas, signifying man's achievements . . . a step into the future, with predictions of constructive things to come. Tomorrow offers new frontiers in science, adventure, and ideals: the Atomic Age . . . the challenge of outer space . . . and the hope for a peaceful and unified world."

Today, Tomorrowland, with its whirling spaceships, zooming rocket vehicles, lush vegetation, and kinetic sculptures and fountains, builds upon Walt Disney's original vision and presents an exciting look beyond the stars to a future full of promise and hope.

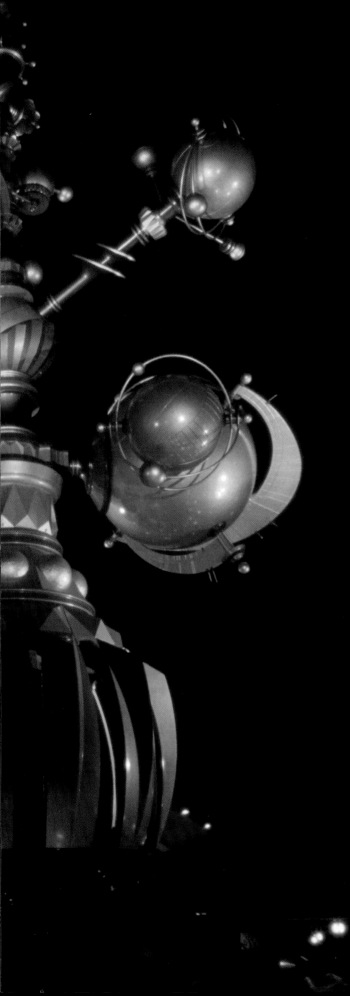

Aboard the Astro Orbiter, guests pilot their own spaceships through a fantastic animated "astronomical model" of planets and constellations. Its colorful rockets circling a series of moving planets, the Astro Orbiter is a radiant and impressive cosmos of colors in tones of burnished copper and brass. The Astro Orbiter welcomes guests at the entrance to Tomorrowland and, both day and night, is an impressive futuristic backdrop to their visits.

169

Honey, I Shrunk the Audience

Honey, I Shrunk the Audience is a hilarious 3-D film experience that gives guests to the Imagination Institute a change of perspective. Join noted Professor Wayne Szalinski as he is honored as the "Inventor of the Year." But things get a little out of control and the audience is ultimately "shrunk" by one of Szalinski's inventions.

Disneyland Monorail™

The Disneyland Monorail, designated "a National Historic Mechanical Engineering Landmark," was the very first daily operating monorail in the Western Hemisphere when it opened in 1959. Since then it has transported thousands of guests along its 2.4-mile "highway in the sky," providing round-trip transportation from the high-tech world of Tomorrowland to the comfort of the Disneyland Resort hotels.

Innoventions®

Innoventions is a two-level interactive pavilion that brings near-future high technology into the world of today. Featuring products and concepts from the world's leading industries, it is divided into five main technology sections: Sports/Recreation, Home, Entertainment, Workplace, and Transportation. After enjoying the interactive first half of the attraction, guests flow to a center atrium where they ascend to the upper-level concept presentations, all clustered around an impressive illuminated tree that is literally "wired" for the future.

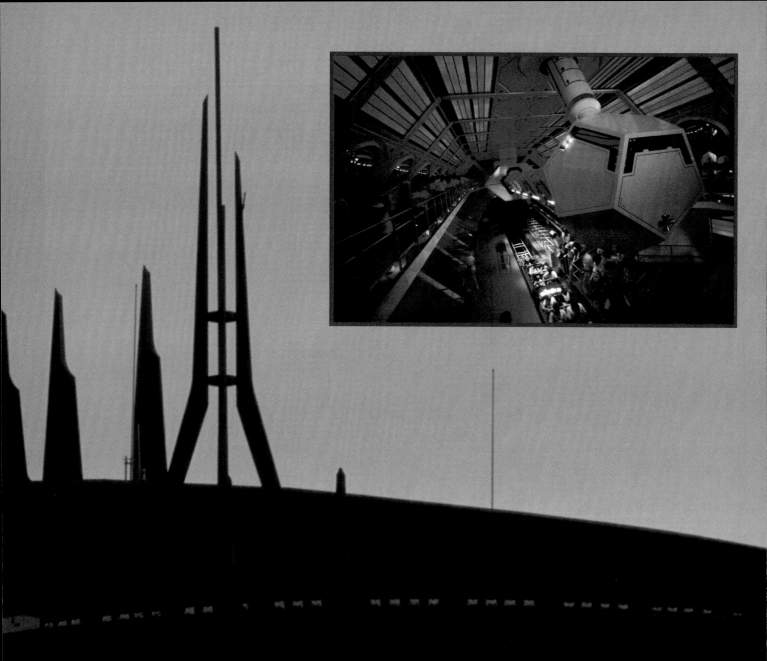

Space Mountain

Under its metallic spires of green and copper, Space Mountain
hosts a thrilling, high-speed adventure through deep space. An
energetic and heart-pounding onboard soundtrack blasts in
the background as guests on this out-of-this-world journey
are whisked through the darkness of outer space, past giant
meteors and shooting stars, and eventually returned after a
hair-raising re-entry to the spaceport.

Star Tours

Inside Star Tours, a bustling inter-galactic travel agency leads guests to a spaceport where they quickly board a StarSpeeder 3000 for a perilous journey to the moon of Endor. Based on George Lucas's famed film series, Star Tours takes its passengers on a harrowing trip through the cosmos, guided by Rex (a rookie pilot), R2-D2, and C-3PO. Along the way, passengers brave a wild trip through comets, narrowly escape an inter-galactic dogfight, and successfully maneuver through the dangerous chasms of a Death Star.

BEHIND THE SCENES

In the Star Tours queue area, guests can hear the announcement: "Mr. Egroeg Sacul, please see the Star Tours agent at gate number 3." Egroeg Sacul is George Lucas spelled backward.

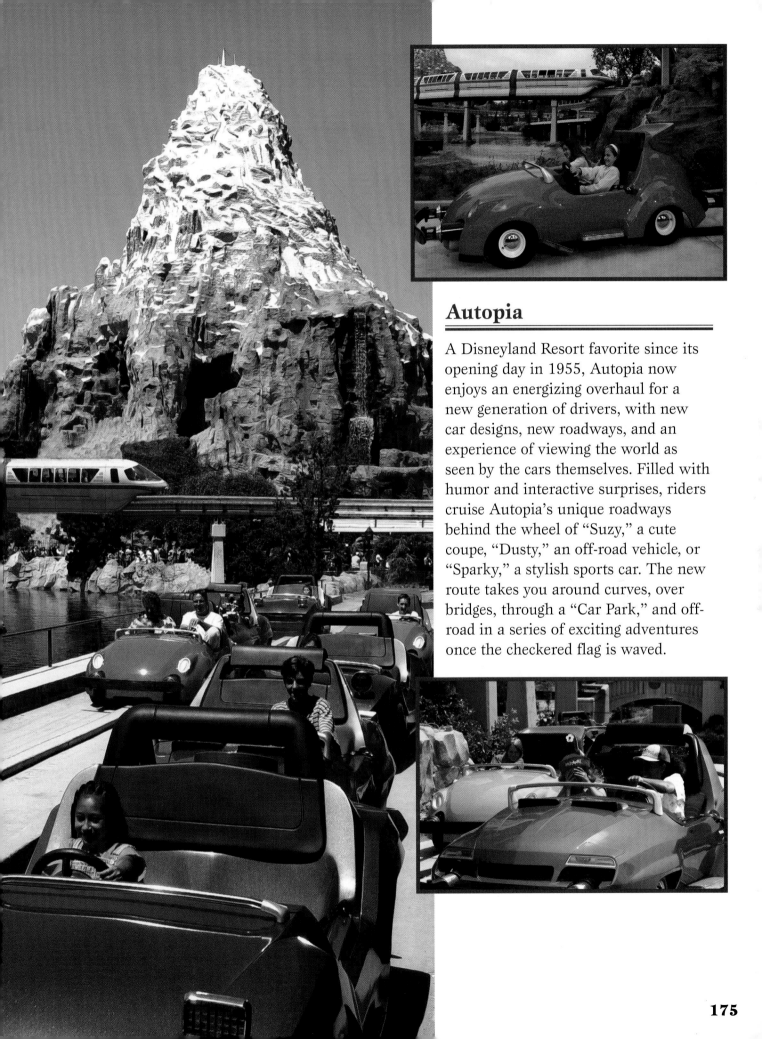

Autopia

A Disneyland Resort favorite since its opening day in 1955, Autopia now enjoys an energizing overhaul for a new generation of drivers, with new car designs, new roadways, and an experience of viewing the world as seen by the cars themselves. Filled with humor and interactive surprises, riders cruise Autopia's unique roadways behind the wheel of "Suzy," a cute coupe, "Dusty," an off-road vehicle, or "Sparky," a stylish sports car. The new route takes you around curves, over bridges, through a "Car Park," and off-road in a series of exciting adventures once the checkered flag is waved.